IRIS
folding

Veel plezier

Maruscha Gaasenbeek
Tine Beauveser

FORTE PUBLISHERS

Contents

© 2004 Forte Uitgevers, Utrecht
© 2004 for the translation by the publisher
Original title: *IRISvouwen speelse vormen*

Sixth printing, July 2005
ISBN 90 5877 377 9

This is a publication from
Forte Publishers BV
P.O. Box 1394
3500 BJ Utrecht
The Netherlands

For more information about the creative books available from Forte Publishers:
www.forteuitgevers.nl

Publisher: Marianne Perlot
Editor: Hanny Vlaar
Photography and digital image editing: Fotografie Gerhard Witteveen, Apeldoorn, the Netherlands
Cover and inner design:
BADE creatieve communicatie, Baarn, the Netherlands
Translation: TextCase, Hilversum, the Netherlands

Preface

With IRIS folding, all the strips of paper encircle a shiny centre. In order to make the patterns look different each time, we can use envelopes, IRIS folding paper and, for special cards, IRIS folding paper de luxe. At our demonstration days that take place all over the country, however, we also saw cards made from strips of origami paper, flower paper, wrapping paper, magazines, advertising pamphlets, flower bulb and clothing catalogues, holographic paper, ribbon, quilt fabric, plaited strips, lining fabric, thin wall paper and even strips cut from plastic carrier bags. With IRIS folding, it is important to be able to choose from many different colours. It is fun to try new combinations every time: one time, for example, red together with burgundy, orange and yellow and the next time blue together with purple, lilac and even pink. The shapes look nice if they are used with matching colours, but you should sometimes try less obvious colour combinations. You will be amazed by the attractive, striking results.

The new patterns used in **Colourful IRISfolding**, such as parasols, caps and glasses of fizzy drinks, are ideal for striking colour combinations. Therefore, our advice is to look through your paper collection and don't be afraid to try something different.

Good luck.

Maruscha   *Tine*

Thanks: to all the loyal fans for their great enthusiasm for IRIS folding.

Techniques

The starting point for IRIS folding is the shape. Cut the shape out of card and then fill the hole from the outside to the inside with folded strips of paper. You work at the back of the card, so you work, in fact, on a mirror image. When you have finished the IRIS folding, stick the card onto another card. For a square shape, select four different sheets of paper where the patterns and colours combine and contrast each other nicely. Cut all the paper into strips in the same way, for example, from left to right. The number of different strips you will need depends on the pattern; you will need between four and eight strips. The width of the strips also depends on the pattern and is stated for each card. You must first fold the edge of each strip over and then sort them into each different type. Next, cover each section in turn by following the numbers (1, 2, 3, 4, 5, etc.), so that the pattern is continuously rotated. Lay the strips down with the fold facing towards the middle of the pattern and stick the left and right-hand sides to the card using adhesive tape. Finally, use an attractive piece of holographic paper to cover the hole in the middle.

The basic shape
(see the bottom right-hand corner of page 5 and card 1 on page 9)

It is important to start with the basic shape, because from this, you will learn the unique folding and sticking technique needed for all the patterns. You will notice that you quickly get used to the technique of IRIS folding.

Preparation

1. Lay a piece of white card (13.8 x 10 cm) down with the back facing towards you.
2. With the aid of a light box, copy the basic shape onto the card using a pencil and cut it out.
3. Stick a copy of the basic pattern given in this book (pattern 1) to your cutting mat using adhesive tape.
4. Place the card with the hole on the pattern (you should be looking at the back of the card) and only stick the left-hand side of the card to your cutting mat using masking tape.
5. Choose four sheets of beige and brown paper, each with different patterns. Two envelopes and two sheets of IRIS folding paper have been used for the card in the bottom right-hand corner of page 5.
6. Cut 2 cm wide strips from these pieces of paper and make separate piles of colour A, colour B, colour C and colour D.
7. Fold the edge of each strip over

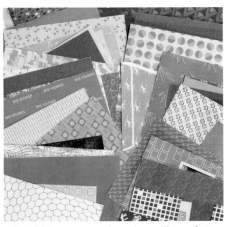

1. IRIS folding paper and envelopes: the perfect combination.

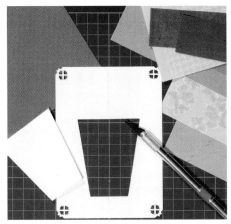

2. Cut the basic shape out of the back of the card. Cut the IRIS folding paper into strips and fold the edge over.

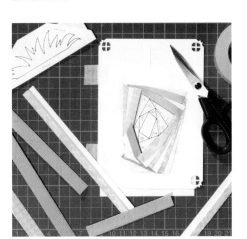

3. Stick the pattern to your cutting mat. Place the card on top and tape the left-hand side to the cutting mat. Place the fold of the strips exactly against the line and stick down the left and right-hand sides using adhesive tape.

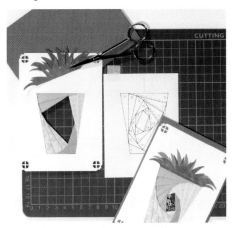

4. Fold the card open from time to time to see whether the pattern you have made continues nicely.

(approximately 0.7 cm wide) *with the nice side facing outwards.*

IRIS folding

8. Take a folded strip of colour A and place it over section 1, exactly against the line of the pattern with the folded edge facing towards the middle. Allow 0.5 cm to stick out on the left and right-hand sides and cut off the rest. By doing so, the strip will also slightly stick out over the edge of the pattern at the bottom, so that section 1 is totally covered.
9. Stick the strip to the card on the left and right-hand sides using a small piece of adhesive tape, but remain 0.5 cm from the edge of the card.
10. Take a strip of colour B and place it on section 2 of the pattern. Tape the left and right-hand sides to the card.
11. Take a strip of colour C. Place this on section 3 and stick it into place.
12. Take a strip of colour D. Place this on section 4 and stick it into place.
13. Start again with colour A on section 5, colour B on section 6, colour C on section 7 and colour D on section 8.

The strips on sections 1, 5, 9, 13 and 17 of this pattern are all of colour A. The strips on sections 2, 6, 10, 14 and 18 are all of colour B. The strips on sections 3, 7, 11, 15 and 19 are all of colour C. The strips on sections 4, 8, 12, 16 and 20 are all of colour D.

Finishing

Carefully remove the card after finishing section 20. Stick a piece of holographic paper in the middle on the back of the card. You can use punches, corner scissors and bits of paper to add extra finishing touches to the card. Stick small pieces of double-sided adhesive tape along the edges. Remove the protective layer and stick your design on a double card. Do not use glue, because all the paper strips place pressure on the card.

Embossing

To emboss, place the stencil on the good side of the card and stick it in place using masking tape. Place the card (with the stencil) upside-down on a light box. Carefully push the paper through the stencil's opening using the embossing stylus. You only have to push along the edges to raise the entire image.
Rub the point of the embossing stylus with a candle so that it glides smoothly over the paper.

Materials

To make the cards:
- Card: Canson Mi-Teintes (C), Artoz (A) and Papicolor (P)
- Separating sheets from K&Company
- IRIS folding text stickers
- IRIS folding greetings sheets
- Knife and cutting mat
- Ruler with a metal cutting edge (Securit)
- Adhesive tape
- Double-sided adhesive tape
- Masking tape
- Various punches (TomTas, Make Me!, Media)
- Various corner punches (Fiskars, Reuser, Lim)
- 2-in-1 border punch (Media)
- Border ornament punches

- 3-in-1 corner punch (Fiskars)
- Punch with exchangeable shapes (TomTas)
- Scissors and silhouette scissors
- Corner scissors (Fiskars)
- Figure scissors (Fiskars, Reuser)
- Embossing stencils (Marianne Design)
- Embossing light box
- Embossing stylus
- Candle
- Ornare pricking template (Marianne Design)
- Pricking mat and pricking pen
- Vellum
- Ridge Master
- Black fine-liner and a pencil
- Photo glue

IRIS folding
- Strips of used envelopes
- Strips of IRIS folding paper
- Strips of IRIS folding paper de luxe

The middle of the card
- Holographic paper

The patterns
Full-size examples of all the patterns are given in this book. Use a light box to draw round the outside. The shapes are usually easy to cut out of the card. Special punched cards are available for the cat, the dog, the small feeding bottle, the jug and the four-leaf clover.

Basic shape

Colourful cards with

bright flower pots.

All the cards are made according to the instructions given for the basic shape (see Techniques).

Card 1
Card: light Havana C502 (14.8 x 21 cm) and white (13.8 x 10 cm) • Pattern 1 • 2 cm wide strips from 2 beige envelopes and 2 sheets of IRIS folding paper (yellow set) • 2 pieces of green paper (3 x 10 cm) for the plant • Gold holographic paper • 3-in-1 corner punch (flower)
Punch the corners of the white card and cut out the pot. Fill the pot with strips. Copy the plant onto a piece of green paper (see page 32). Place the second piece of green paper on the other piece of paper and staple them together. Cut the plants out and stick them above the pot .

Card 2
Card: Structura sunflower P134 (14.8 x 21 cm), cornflower A425 (13.7 x 9.5 cm) and white (13.3 x 9 cm) • Pattern 1 • 4 groups of 2 cm wide strips from 3 yellow envelopes • Piece of grey

envelope paper (6 x 9 cm) • 2 cm wide yellow strips of IRIS folding paper de luxe (pastels set) • Gold holographic paper • Figure scissors (heartstrings) • Flowers from a hand punch
Use the figure scissors to cut the strips of IRIS folding paper de luxe into 1 cm wide strips. Lay one half aside and add the other half to the

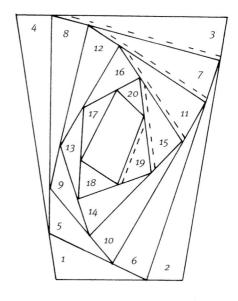

Pattern 1, basic shape

1.

2.

3.

4.

5.

6.

group of colour C. Place the yellow strips up to the dotted line and then place the strips cut with the figure scissors on top up to the line of section 3. Also do this for sections 7, 11, 15 and 19.

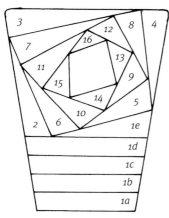

Pattern 2, glass

Card 3

Card: brick red P35 (14.8 x 21 cm) and white (14.1 x 9.6 cm) • Pattern 1 • 2 cm wide strips from four sheets of IRIS folding paper (green, orange and yellow sets) • Green paper for the plant (3 x 10 cm) • Gold holographic paper • Corner punch (spear) • Figure punch (flower) • Punch (small flower)

Card 4

Card: ivory C111 (14.8 x 21 cm) and brick red P35 (13.7 x 9.4 cm) • Pattern 1 • 2 cm wide strips from 4 sheets of IRIS folding paper (orange and yellow sets) • Silver holographic paper • Photo corner figure punch (flower) • Punch (flower)
After completing the IRIS folding, punch the corners of the ivory card and slide the red card behind the flowers.

Card 5

Card: cornflower A425 (14.8 x 21 cm) and Structura fresh green P130 (13.6 x 9.5 cm) • Pattern 1 • 2 cm wide strips from 4 lilac envelopes • 2 cm wide strips of IRIS folding paper de luxe (bright set) • Green paper for the branches • Silver holographic paper • 3-in-1 corner punch (leaves) • Figure punch (waves) • Figure punch (branch)

Card 6

Card: cerise P33 (14.8 x 21 cm), Antica green P169 (14.3 x 10 cm) and white (13.8 x 9.5 cm) • Pattern 1 • 2 cm wide strips from 4 sheets of IRIS folding paper (red, orange and petrol sets) • Petrol paper (3 x 6 cm) for the cactus • Silver holographic paper • Corner scissors (regal) • Punch (strawberry)

Playing with shapes

The jug is full, so fill

the glasses.

The glasses are made according to the instructions given for card 1 and the jug is made according to the instructions given for card 2.

Card 1
Card: lilac A453 (14.8 x 21 cm), pastel green A331 (14.5 x 10 cm and 0.35 x 5 cm for the straws) and white (13.8 x 9.8 cm) • Pattern 2 • 2 cm wide strips from 2 sheets of IRIS folding paper (purple and aqua sets) • Silver holographic paper • Fruit from a fruits-of-the-forest teabag • Corner punch (flower)

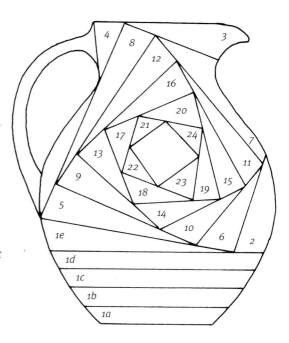

Pattern 3, drinks jug

Punch two corners of the white card. Cut out the glasses and fill them with the strips. Make a 0.7 cm long incision at the top of each glass for the straws and stick them in place.

Card 2

Card: lobster red A545 (13 x 26 cm), sienna C374 (11.5 x 11.5 cm) and white (10.5 x 10.5 cm) • *Pattern 3* • *2 cm wide strips from 3 sheets of IRIS folding paper (orange set) and 1 sheet of IRIS folding paper de luxe (bright set)* • *Piece of IRIS folding paper de luxe (bright set) (11 x 11 cm)* • *Gold holographic paper* • *Die-cut stickers (K&Company)*

Cut the jug, but not the handle, out of the white card. Cut the handle out of orange paper.

Card 3

Card: Structura sunflower P134 (14.8 x 21 cm), orange (14 x 9.9 cm) and Structura pale yellow P132 (14 x 9.3 cm) • *Pattern 2* • *2 cm wide strips from 1 orange envelope, 2 sheets of IRIS folding paper (yellow set) and 1 sheet of IRIS folding paper de luxe (pastels set)* • *Gold holographic paper* • *3-in-1 corner punch (celestial)* • *Lemon from a lemon-flavour teabag* • *Paper (4.5 x 0.4 cm) for the straw* • *Bubbles from the art punch*

Card 4

Card: pink A481 (14.8 x 21 cm), violet C507 (14 x 10 cm) and white C335 (13 x 9.5 cm) • *Pattern 2* • *2 cm wide strips from 4 sheets of IRIS folding paper (red and purple sets)* • *2 pieces of IRIS*

1.

3.

4.

6.

folding paper de luxe (pastels set) for the straws (0.35 x 5 cm) and the lemon (Ø 2 cm) • Gold holographic paper • 3-in-1 corner punch (celestial)

Card 5
Card: ivory C111 (14.8 x 21 cm and 10.5 x 10.5 cm) and bright yellow C400 (13.9 x 10.5 cm) • Pattern 3 • 2 cm wide strips from 1 yellow envelope, 2 sheets of IRIS folding paper (yellow set) and 1 sheet of de luxe IRIS folding paper (pastels set) • Gold holographic paper • Figure punch (flower)

Card 6
Card: cerise P33 (14.8 x 21 cm), warm yellow C553 (13.9 x 9.8 cm) and white C110 (13.5 x 9.4 cm) • Pattern 2 • 2 cm wide strips from 3 orange/red/ pink envelopes and 1 sheet of IRIS folding paper de luxe (bright set) • Rainbow holographic paper • 3-in-1 corner punch (flowers) • Orange from a orange-flavour teabag • Half a straw

Card 7
Card: fiesta red P12 (13 x 26 cm) and white (11.5 x 11.5 cm) • Pattern 3 • 2 cm wide strips from 1 orange envelope and 3 sheets of IRIS folding paper (orange set) • K&Company Romanza ivory embossed paper (12.2 x 12.2 cm) • Silver holographic paper • Border punch (spring)

Parasol

All the parasols are made according to the instructions given for card 1.

Card 1

Card: royal blue A427 (14.8 x 21 cm) and Structura orange P135 (14.8 x 10 cm) •
Pattern 4 • 4 groups of 2 cm wide strips from 3 blue envelopes • Silver holographic paper
• Figure scissors (heartstrings) • Figure punch (shell)
Use the figure scissors to cut along two edges of the small card. Cut out the parasol without the pole. To make the twinshell, place a folded piece of paper in the punch so that the fold almost touches the top of the shell. Cut the pole out of paper and stick it on the card together with the shells.

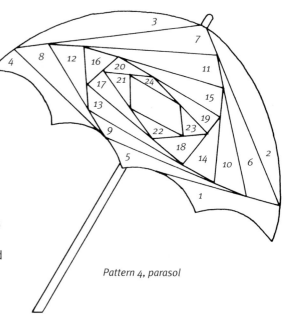

Pattern 4, parasol

Card 2

Card: IRIS blue P31 (13 x 26 cm), green (12.2 x 12.2 cm) and white (11.5 x 11.5 cm)
• Pattern 4 • 2 cm wide strips from blue/green envelopes • Silver holographic paper
• Embossing stencil (corners) • IRIS folding text sticker

Card 3

Card: sunny yellow A247 (14.8 x 21 cm), lemon C101 (13.6 x 10.2 cm) and cornflower blue A425 (13 x 10 cm) • Pattern 4 • 2 cm wide strips from 2 orange envelopes and 2 sheets of IRIS folding paper (yellow and orange sets) • Gold holographic paper • 3-in-1 corner punch (celestial)

Card 4

Card: fiesta red P12 (13 x 26 cm), sunny yellow A247 (12 x 12 cm) and Structura pale yellow P132 (11.6 x 11.6 cm) • Pattern 4 • 2 cm wide strips from one envelope and 3 sheets of IRIS folding paper (red, orange and yellow sets) • Gold holographic paper • IRIS folding text sticker • Border ornament punch (wave)

Card 5

Card: lobster red A545 (13 x 26 cm), Structura fern green P137 (12 x 12 cm) and white (11.8 x

11.8 cm) • Pattern 4 • 2 cm wide strips from 4 sheets of IRIS folding paper (yellow and orange sets) • Silver holographic paper • Embossing stencil (garden) • Background embossing stencil AE 1201 • Punch (shell)

Card 6

Card: IRIS blue P31 (13 x 26 cm), apple green C475 (11.6 x 11.6 cm) and Structura fresh green P130 (11 x 11 cm) • Pattern 4 • 2 cm wide strips from 2 reddish brown and blue envelopes, 1 sheet of IRIS folding paper (yellow set) and 1 purple IRIS folding greetings sheet • Gold holographic paper

Card 7

Card: yellow A275 (14.8 x 21 cm) and violet P20 (13.5 x 10 cm) • Pattern 4 • 2 cm wide strips from 2 envelopes and 2 sheets of IRIS folding paper (yellow set) • Gold holographic paper • IRIS folding text sticker • Border ornament punch (rope)

1.

2.

3.

4.

5.

6.

Cats and dogs

Cuddly, trustworthy friends

for young and old.

The cat is made according to the instructions given for card 1 and the dog is made according to the instructions given for card 2. Use a light box to copy the eyes, mouth and nose with a black fine-liner.

Card 1 (on the cover)
Card: salmon C384 (13 x 26 cm), Structura orange P135 (12 x 12 cm) and white C335 (11 x 11 cm) • Pattern 5 • 2 cm wide strips from 4 sheets of IRIS folding paper (orange and yellow sets) • Colour B (3 x 4 cm) for the head • Gold holographic paper • 3-in-1 corner punch (bugs) Punch the top corners of the white card and cut out the body without the head and the tail. Fill the body with the strips of paper. Stick the other parts to the body.

Card 2
Card: white C335 (13 x 26 cm and 13 x 11.8 cm), dark chestnut C501 (12. 7 x 12.7 cm) and Havana brown C502 (12.3 x 12.3 cm) • Pattern 6 • 2 cm wide strips from 3 brown envelopes and

1 sheet of IRIS folding paper (yellow set) • Brown paper (3 x 4 cm) for the head • Gold holographic paper • Border punch (rope) Punch the edges of the small white card and cut out the body without the head and the tail. Note: colour A stops after section 17!

Pattern 5, cat

Card 3

Card: bright red C506 (13 x 26 cm and 11.8 x 11.8 cm), gold P102 (12.5 x 12.5 cm) and white C335 (11.5 x 11.5 cm) • Pattern 5 • 2 cm wide strips from 4 grey envelopes • Grey paper (3 x 4 cm) for the head • Gold holographic paper • 3-in-1 corner punch (hearts)

Card 4

Card: sandy yellow C407 (13 x 26 cm) and cerise P33 (11.5 x 11.5 cm) • Pattern 6 • 4 groups of 2 cm wide strips from 3 beige/ yellow envelopes • Pale green envelope paper (12 x 12 cm) • Yellow paper (3 x 4 cm) for the head • Gold holographic paper • Puppies from a hand punch • Bones from a border punch

Card 5

Card: white (13 x 26 cm), rust C504 (12.7 x 12.7 cm) and salmon C384 (12.4 x 12.4 cm) • Pattern 5 • 2 cm wide strips from 4 reddish orange envelopes • Red envelope paper (3 x 4 cm) for the head • Bronze holographic paper • 2-in-1 border punch (paw)

Card 6

Card: brick red P35 (13 x 26 cm), metallic bronze (12.1 x 12.1 cm)

and white C335 (11.5 x 11.5 cm) • Pattern 6 • 2 cm wide strips from 2 brown envelopes and 2 sheets of IRIS folding paper (yellow and orange sets) • Gold holographic paper • IRIS folding text sticker

Pattern 6, dog

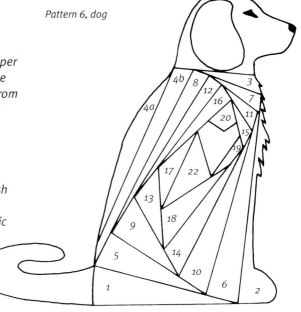

Windmill

A fresh wind

turns the sails.

All the cards are made according to the instructions given for card 1.

Card 1

Card: brick red P35 (13 x 26 cm) and white C111 (12.4 x 12.2 cm) • Pattern 7 • 2 cm wide strips from 1 yellow envelope, 2 sheets of IRIS folding paper (yellow and orange sets) and 1 sheet of IRIS folding paper de luxe (flowers set) • Bronze holographic paper • Border ornament punch (heart) • Small hearts from a corner punch (hearts)

Punch the top corners of the white card and cut out the main part of the windmill. Fill the windmill with strips as described for the basic shape.

Copy the top of the windmill and stick it 0.4 cm above the windmill. Staple together four strips of yellow envelope paper (2 x 8 cm) and a copy of one windmill sail. Cut the four sails out at the same time and stick them on the card. Decorate the card with hearts from the punch.

1.

3.

2.

Card 2
Card: bright yellow C400 (13 x 26 cm) and white (12.4 x 12.1 cm) • Pattern 7 • 2 cm wide strips from 3 green envelopes and 1 sheet of IRIS folding paper de luxe (flowers set) • Silver holographic paper • Corner punch (tulip)

Card 3
Card: Structura royal blue P136 (13 x 26 cm) and white (12.5 x 12.5 cm) • Pattern 7 • 2 cm wide strips from 5 blue envelopes • Silver holographic paper • Corner punch (tulip) • Birds from an envelope

Card 4
Card: burgundy (13 x 26 cm), bright red C506 (12.5 x 12.3 cm), white C335 (12.5 x 11.8 cm) and 4 pieces of cerise paper P33 (2 x 8 cm) for the sails • Pattern 7 • 2 cm wide strips from 4 red envelopes • Silver holographic paper • Figure punch (girl) • Balloons from a 2-in-1 border punch • 3-in-1 corner punch (hearts)
To make two girls hand-in-hand, slide a folded piece of paper sideways into the punch until the fold is half way across the second hand.

4.

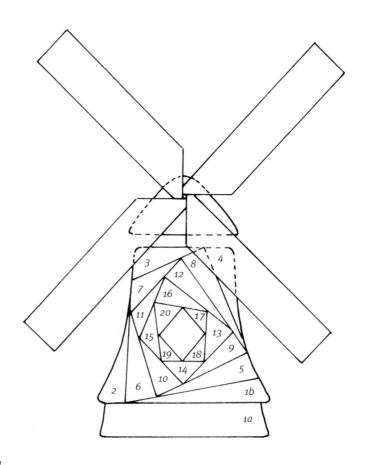

Pattern 7, windmill

Baseball cap

Such a hat

suits everybody.

All the cards are made according to the instructions given for card 1.

Card 1
Card: dark blue A417 (14.8 x 21 cm) and white (13.8 x 9 cm) • Pattern 8 • 2 cm wide strips from 2 blue envelopes and 2 sheets of IRIS folding paper (blue set) • Blue paper (3 x 6 cm) for the peak • Blue IRIS folding paper (14.3 x 9.7 cm) • Red paper (14.6 x 9.7 cm) • Art punch (spear)
Punch the corners of the white card with part of the corner punch and cut out the baseball cap without the peak. Fill the cap with strips. Use a light box to copy the peak and the button. Cut them out and stick them on the card. Stick the card on blue paper, then on red paper and finally on the double card.

Card 2
Card: Structura orange P135 (14.8 x 21 cm) and irisblue P31 (14.2 x 9.9 cm) • Pattern 8 • 2 cm wide strips from 4 orange, grey, blue and greyish blue envelopes • Orange paper (3 x 6 cm) for the

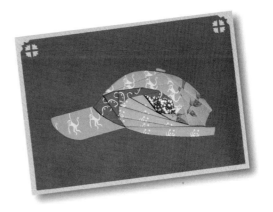

peak • Silver holographic paper • 3-in-1 corner punch (flowers)

Card 3
Card: bright yellow P10 (14.8 x 21 cm) and white (14.3 x 10 cm) • Pattern 8 • 2 cm wide strips from 4 sheets of IRIS folding paper (green and yellow sets) • Yellow paper (3 x 6 cm) for the peak • Gold holographic paper • Border ornament punch (rope) • Punch (car) • IRIS folding text sticker

Card 4
Card: grass green P07 (14.8 x 21 cm), Christmas green P18 (14.1 x 9.8 cm) and white C335 (13.7 x

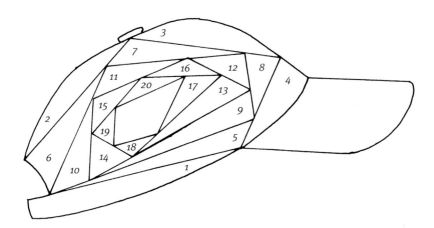

Pattern 8, baseball cap

9.4 cm) • Pattern 8 • 2 cm wide strips from
4 green envelopes • Green paper (3 x 6 cm)
for the peak • Silver holographic paper •
Multi-corner punch

Card 5

Card: dark blue A417 (14.8 x 21 cm), mango
A575 (14.5 x 10 cm) and white C335 (14.2 x
9.7 cm) • Pattern 8 • 2 cm wide strips from
4 yellow, orange and blue envelopes • Blue
paper (3 x 6 cm) for the peak • Silver holographic paper • Embossing stencil (corners)
• Dragonflies from a punch

Card 6

Card: petrol (14.8 x 21 cm) and lavender blue
C150 (13.4 x 9 cm) • Pattern 8 • 2 cm wide strips
from 4 envelopes (white with text, blue, aqua
and green/blue fishbone) • White envelope
paper with text (13.7 x 9.5 cm) • Grey paper
(3 x 6 cm) for the peak • Silver holographic paper

Card 7

Card: white C335 (14.8 x 21 cm and 13.6 x
9.3 cm) • Pattern 8 • 2 cm wide strips from 2
grey envelopes and 2 reddish orange envelopes
• Envelope paper with text for the peak (5 x
4 cm) • Grey envelope (13.9 x 9.6 cm) plus 2
red edges • Silver holographic paper

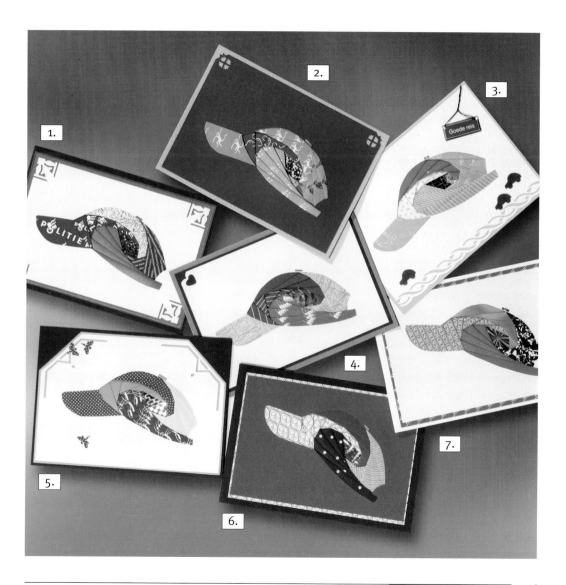

Baby feeding bottles

These baby feeding bottles will soon be hanging on a line in the nursery.

The bottles are made according to the instructions given for card 1 and the large patterns are made according to the instructions given for card 4.

Card 1
Card: pink A481 (13 x 26 cm), red A517 (11 x 11 cm) and white (10.4 x 10.4 cm) • Pattern 9 • 4 groups of 2 cm wide strips from 3 different envelopes • Silver holographic paper • Embossing stencil (baby)
Cut the bottle out of white card without the cap or the teat and emboss the shapes on it. Use a light box to copy the cap and the teat. Cut them out and stick them on the card.

Card 2
Card: mango A575 (13 x 26 cm) and Structura orange P135 (10.5 x 7 cm) • Pattern 9 • 2 cm wide strips from 1 sheet of K&Company Peach Dots paper, 1 sheet of IRIS folding paper (orange set) and 2 sheets of IRIS folding paper de luxe (flowers and pastels sets) • K&Company Peach Dots paper (11.7 x 11.7 cm) • Gold holographic paper • Border ornament punch (sunburst) • Punch (crown)
Place a 1.1 cm wide pink strip of paper in a Ridge Master and then cut it into the shape of the cap.

Card 3
Card: royal blue A427 (14.8 x 21 cm) and white (14 x 9.7 cm and 3.5 x 10 cm) • Pattern 9 • 2 cm wide strips from 4 blue envelopes • Blue IRIS folding greetings sheet (3.2 x 5 cm) • Silver holographic paper • Balloons from a 2-in-1 border punch • Pencil
Fold the small card double so that it measures 3.5 x 5 cm and stick the greetings sheet on it. Use a pencil to draw strings to tie the balloons to.

Card 4
Card: lavender blue C150 (14.8 x 21 cm) and lemon C101 (13.7 x 8.9 cm) • Pattern 10 • 2 cm wide strips from 4 blue envelopes • Blue envelope (2 x 2.5 cm) for the teat • K&Company Romanza citrus paper (14.3 x 9.7 cm) • Silver holographic paper • Corner scissors (celestial) • Figure punch (bear)

Card 5

Card: apricot P24 (14.8 x 21 cm) and pale pink (14.3 x 10 cm) • Pattern 10 • 2 cm wide strips from 2 sheets of IRIS folding paper (orange set) and 2 sheets of IRIS folding paper de luxe (flowers and bright sets)
• Bronze holographic paper • Corner punch (bow) • Baby girl outfit from Crea Motion

Card 6

Card: pink A481 (14.8 x 21 cm) and white (14.3 x 10 cm)
• Pattern 9 • 2 cm wide strips from 2 pink envelopes and 2 sheets of IRIS folding paper (red and purple sets)
• Silver holographic paper
• 3-in-1 corner punch (hearts) • Ridge Master
• Baby girl outfit from Crea Motion

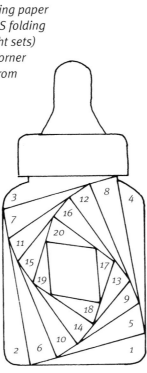

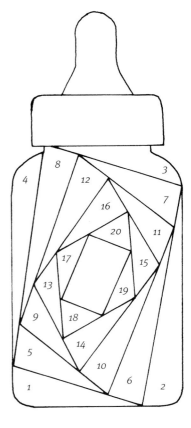

Pattern 9, small feeding bottle   *Pattern 10, large feeding bottle*

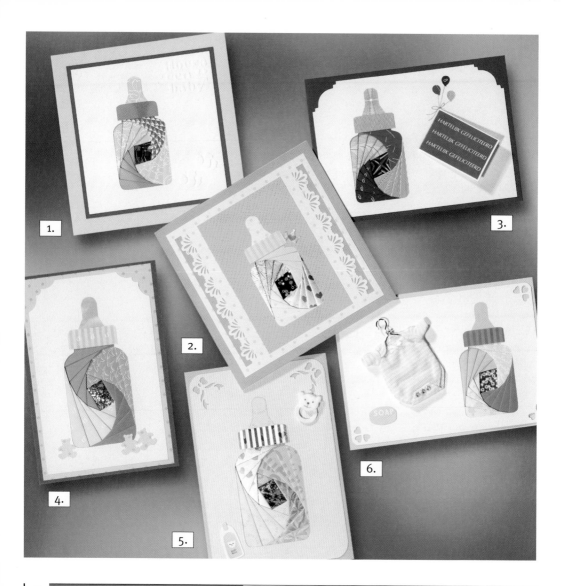

1.

3.

2.

4.

5.

6.

1.

2.

3.

4.

5.

6.

4-leaf clovers and strawberries

Lucky four-leaf clovers

and summer fruit.

The four-leaf clover is made according to the instructions given for card 1 and the strawberry is made according to the instructions given for card 2.

Card 1 (card on the cover)
Card: Structura fresh green P130 (14.8 x 21 cm), Christmas green P18 (13 x 9,5 cm) and white C335 (12.5 x 9 cm) • Pattern 11 • 1 cm wide strips from 3 sheets of IRIS folding paper (green set) and 1 sheet of IRIS folding paper de luxe (pastels set)
• Silver holographic paper • Asian sign punch
Turn the punch upside down and punch part of the pattern in the corners of the white card. Cut out the four leaves and fill them with strips. Cut the stem out of green paper and stick it on the card. Cut two strips (9.5 x 1 cm) from pastel green paper and stick them above and below the second card.

Card 2
Card: lily white C110 (13 x 26 cm and 6.5 x 6.5 cm), wine red C503 (9.6 x 9.6 cm) and brick

red C505 (8.9 x 8.9 cm) • Pattern 12 • 1.5 cm wide strips from 3 sheets of IRIS folding paper (red set) and 1 sheet of IRIS folding paper de luxe (bright set) • Green paper (2.5 x 5 cm)
• Silver holographic paper

Cut the strawberry, but not the top, out of the white card. Fill the strawberry with strips (see Techniques).

Card 3
Card: pale pink C350 (14.8 x 21 cm), rust brown C504 (13.1 x 9.7 cm) and ivory C111 (12.4 x 10.5 cm) • Pattern 11 • 1 cm wide strips from 3 sheets of IRIS folding paper (green and yellow sets) • Gold holographic paper • Border ornament punch (leaves)

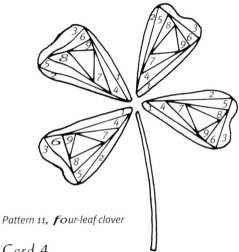

Pattern 11, *fo*ur-leaf clover

Card 4

Card: Stru*ctura pale yellow P132 (14.8 x 21 cm),
metallic *b*rown P144 (12.8 x 8.5 cm) and lemon
C101 (8 x *7* cm) • Pattern 11 • 1 cm wide strips
of IRIS fo *ld*ing paper (green set) • Gold holographic *p*aper • Rounder corner scissors • Art
punch (fl*o*wer)*
Cut the f*o*ur-leaf clover out of the smallest card
and roun *d* off the corners. Punch the corners of
the brow *n* card.

Card 5

Card: wh *ite* (14.8 x 21 cm and 14.8 x 6.5 cm) and
cerise P*3*3 (14.8 x 7.5 cm) • Pattern 12 • 1.5 cm

wide strips from 4 pink/red envelopes • Green
paper (2.5 x 5 cm) • Gold holographic paper
• Ornare pricking template (Fruit PK 035)
• IRIS folding text stickers • Punch (strawberry)

Card 6

Card: red A517 (14.8 x 21 cm) and white (14.3 x
10 cm) • Pattern 12 • 1.5 cm wide strips from
2 red envelopes and 2 sheets of IRIS folding
paper de luxe (Christmas and bright sets) •
Green paper (2.5 x 5 cm) • Wekon ladybird
vellum (14.8 x 21 cm) • Red holographic paper
Cut the frame out of the vellum (9.5 x 7 cm).

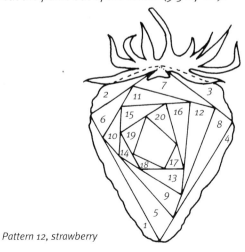

Pattern 12, strawberry

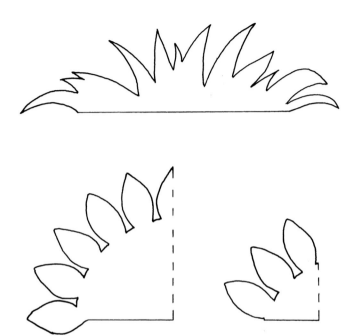

Plant pattern (the basic shape)

Many thanks to:

Kars & Co BV in Ochten, the Netherlands.
Koninklijke Talens in Apeldoorn, the Netherlands for supplying the card

The materials used can be ordered by shopkeepers from:
Avec B.V. in Waalwijk, the Netherlands
Kars & Co BV in Ochten, the Netherlands.